First Drawings

Dogs

BIG BUDDY
FIRST DRAWINGS
BOOKS

Big Buddy Books
An Imprint of Abdo Publishing
abdopublishing.com

By Katie Lajiness

abdopublishing.com

Published by Abdo Publishing, a division of ABDO, PO Box 398166, Minneapolis, Minnesota 55439. Copyright © 2017 by Abdo Consulting Group, Inc. International copyrights reserved in all countries. No part of this book may be reproduced in any form without written permission from the publisher. Big Buddy Books™ is a trademark and logo of Abdo Publishing.

Printed in the United States of America, North Mankato, Minnesota.
092016
012017

THIS BOOK CONTAINS RECYCLED MATERIALS

Illustrations: Michael Jacobsen/Spectrum Studio
Interior Photos: Deposit Photos

Coordinating Series Editor: Tamara L. Britton
Graphic Design: Taylor Higgins, Maria Hosley

Publisher's Cataloging-in-Publication Data

Names: Lajiness, Katie, author.
Title: Dogs / by Katie Lajiness.
Description: Minneapolis, MN : Abdo Publishing, 2017. | Series: First drawings |
    Includes index.
Identifiers: LCCN 2016945190 | ISBN 9781680785234 (lib. bdg.) |
    ISBN 9781680798838 (ebook)
Subjects: LCSH: Dogs in art--Juvenile literature. | Drawing--Technique--
    Juvenile literature.
Classification: DDC 743.6/9772--dc23
LC record available at http://lccn.loc.gov/2016945190

Table of Contents

Getting Started

Today, you're going to draw dogs. Not sure you know how to draw? Dogs are easy to **sketch** if you break them down into circles, ovals, rectangles, squares, and triangles.

To begin, you'll need paper, a sharpened pencil, a big eraser, and a flat surface. Draw each shape lightly. When these **guidelines** are light, it is easy to erase and try again.

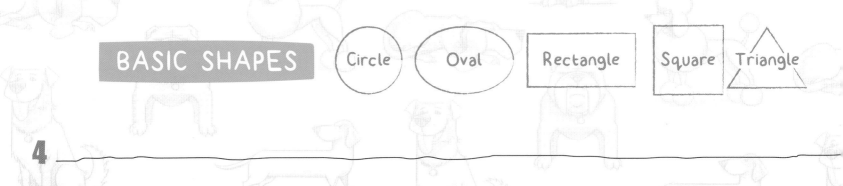

BASIC SHAPES   Circle   Oval   Rectangle   Square   Triangle

Wiener Dog

Sleepy Dog

Poodle

Bulldog

Happy Dog

5

Adding Color

Once you learn to draw an object, you may want to add color. Let's learn how to mix colors and add shading.

Shading

MARKERS
Use similar colors to create shading.

PENCILS AND CRAYONS
Use less pressure for lighter shades and more pressure for darker shades.

PAINTS
Add white to lighten and black or blue to darken shades.

There are three primary colors. They are red, yellow, and blue. These colors cannot be made by mixing other colors. However, you can make many colors by mixing primary colors together.

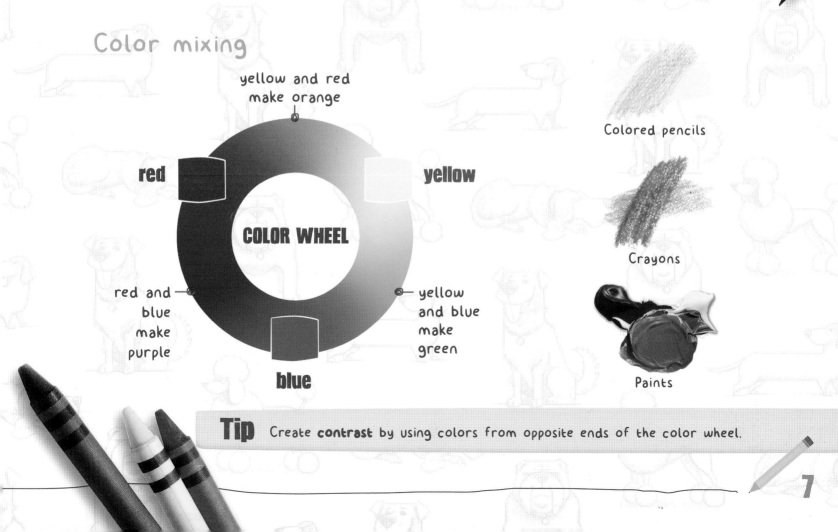

Color mixing

yellow and red make orange

red

yellow

COLOR WHEEL

red and blue make purple

yellow and blue make green

blue

Colored pencils

Crayons

Paints

Tip Create **contrast** by using colors from opposite ends of the color wheel.

Wiener Dog

Let's learn to draw a wiener dog!

STEP 1

Draw basic circle, rectangle, and triangle **guidelines** for the head, snout, neck, body, and legs. **Sketch** ovals for the paws.

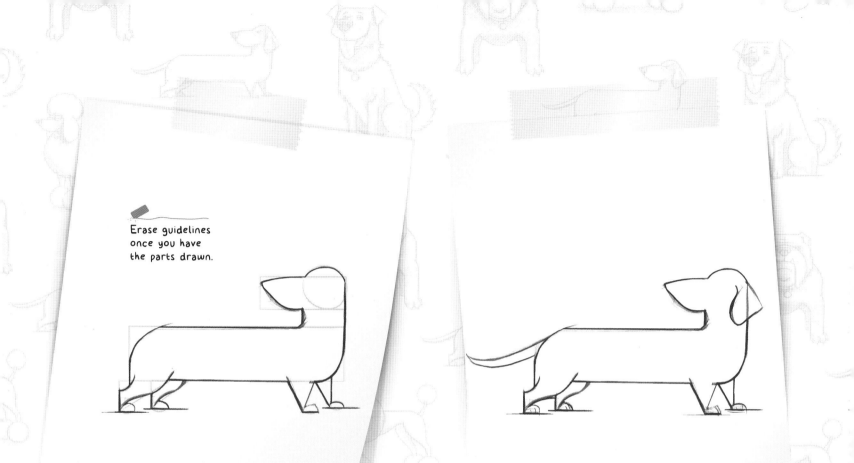

Erase guidelines once you have the parts drawn.

Connect the shapes to form the dog's **outline**.

Sketch body features such as a tail and ear. Add **details** to the paws.

STEP 4

Draw in the dog's eye, nose, and eyebrow.

STEP 5

Create **texture** and style by adding shading.

It's time for some color! You can add your own color and shading to personalize your drawing.

Poodle

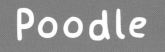

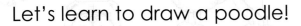

Let's learn to draw a poodle!

Draw basic circle, triangle, and oval **guidelines** for the head, snout, body, and legs.

Erase guidelines
once you have
the parts drawn.

Connect the shapes to form the
dog's **outline**.

Add body features such as a tail,
ears, eyes, and nose. Make the
poodle look fluffy by adding fur.

STEP 4

Now add the poodle's collar and tag.

STEP 5

Create **texture** and shape by adding shading to your poodle.

STEP 6

It's time for some color! You can add your own color and shading to personalize your drawing.

YOU DID IT!

Well done! You drew a poodle.

15

Sleepy Dog

Let's learn to draw a sleepy dog!

Draw basic oval, rectangle, and triangle **guidelines** for the head, snout, body, and legs.

Erase guidelines
once you have
the parts drawn.

STEP 2

Connect the shapes to form the dog's **outline**.

STEP 3

Draw in the ear and tail. Add **details** to the paws.

STEP 4

Sketch in the collar, eyes, and nose.

STEP 5

Create depth and shape by adding shading to your sleepy dog.

It's time for some color! You can add your own color and shading to personalize your drawing.

YOU DID IT!

Congratulations! You drew a sleepy dog.

Bulldog

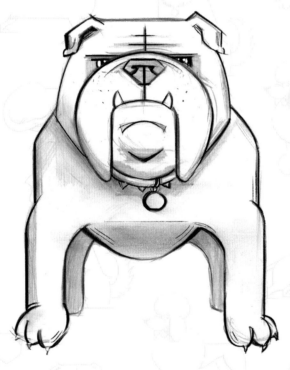

Let's learn to draw a bulldog!

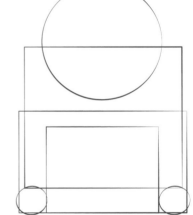

STEP 1

Draw basic circle and rectangle **guidelines** for the head, body, legs, and paws.

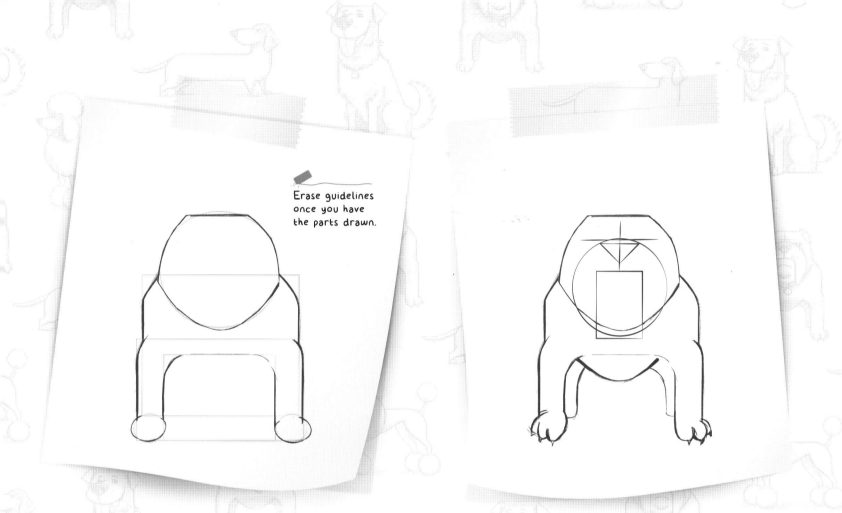

Erase guidelines
once you have
the parts drawn.

Connect the shapes to form the
dog's **outline**.

Add body features such as a belly,
paws, and hind legs. **Sketch** light
guidelines across the dog's face.

Erase guidelines once you have the parts drawn.

Use **guidelines** to draw the eyes, nose, mouth, and jowls. Add ears, a collar, and tag.

Add more **details** such as forehead wrinkles and teeth. Create **texture** and shape by adding shading.

STEP 6

It's time for some color! You can add your own color and shading to personalize your drawing.

YOU DID IT!

Yippee! You drew a bulldog.

Happy Dog

Let's learn to draw a happy dog!

Draw basic oval **guidelines** for the head, neck, body, legs, and paws.

24

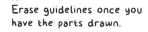
Erase guidelines once you have the parts drawn.

Connect the shapes to form the dog's **outline**.

Add playful ears and a tail to your happy dog.

Start your dog's face by drawing its snout.

Add face **details** such as the nose, tongue, and mouth.

STEP 6

Draw in your dog's eyes and finish the face.

STEP 7

Make your happy dog look fluffy by adding fur. Add **details** to the paws.

Draw a collar and tag.

Create **texture** and style by adding shading to your dog.

Tools There are many tools you can use to add color such as crayons, colored pencils, paints, or markers.

YOU DID IT!

Yay! You drew a happy dog.

STEP 10

It's time for some color! You can add your own color and shading to personalize your drawing.

On Your Own

To build your drawing skills, practice finding basic shapes in everyday objects. Finding basic shapes can help you draw almost anything. Use what you've learned to draw other dogs. The more you draw, the better you will be!

Glossary

contrast the amount of difference in color or brightness.

depth measurement from top to bottom or from front to back.

detail a minor decoration, such as a dog's whiskers.

guideline a rule or instruction that shows or tells how something should be done.

outline the outer edges of a shape.

sketch to make a rough drawing.

texture the look or feel of something.

Websites

To learn more about First Drawings, visit **booklinks.abdopublishing.com**. These links are routinely monitored and updated to provide the most current information available.

Index